W9-BYP-610

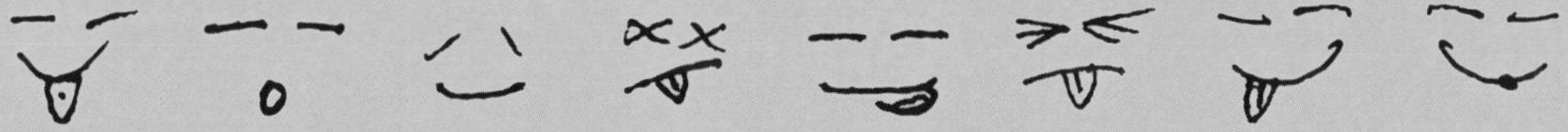

Eight Little Faces

A Mom's Journey

By Kate Gosselin

Eight Little Faces
Copyright © 2009 by Katie Gosselin

Requests for information should be addressed to:
Zondervan, *Grand Rapids, Michigan 49530*

ISBN 978-0-310-31846-0

All Scripture quotations, unless otherwise indicated, are taken from the *Holy Bible, Today's New International Version.*™, TNIV®
Copyright © 2001, 2005 by International Bible Society®. Used by permission of Zondervan. All rights reserved worldwide.

Scripture references marked ESV are taken from *The Holy Bible English Standard Version*, copyright © 2001 by Good News
Publishers. Used by permission. All rights reserved.

Internet addresses (websites, blogs, etc.) and telephone numbers printed in this book are offered as a resource to you. These are
not intended in any way to be or imply an endorsement on the part of Zondervan, nor do we vouch for the content of these sites
and numbers for the life of this book.

All rights reserved. No part of this publication may be reproduced, stored in a retrieval system, or transmitted in any form or by
any means—electronic, mechanical, photocopy, recording, or any other—except for brief quotations in printed reviews, without
the prior permission of the publisher.

Photos provided by the Gosselin Family

Interior Design by Steve Culver

Printed in the United States of America

09 10 11 12 • 5 4 3 2 1

Dedicated to the eight little faces I get
to greet each and every morning —
the faces that make me smile on a rough
day; that carry me through as much
as I carry them through. I love you more
than words can describe, Cara, Madelyn,
Alexis, Hannah, Aaden, Collin, Leah, and
Joel. Thanks for teaching me the depths
of a mother's love!

Dreams

A WORD FROM KATE

As a little girl, I used to dream that there was a surplus of babies in the world who needed a mommy and one would be left on my doorstep. I realized then that more than anything else in my life, I wanted to be a mom.

R

Take delight in the Lord and he will give you the desires of your heart.

Psalm 37:4

When Jon and I learned I had fertility issues, we were devastated. I finally became pregnant after going to a fertility specialist but had no idea how completely our prayers had been answered. I held my breath as the ultrasound started and sobbed with pure delight when I heard it: two babies! God had doubly blessed us!

Ask and you will receive, and your joy will be complete.

John 16:24

b

Finally, I was somebody's mom ... well, two somebodies! Those first three years as a little family were nothing short of pure bliss. Watching our two little girls grow and change was beyond amazing, and I enjoyed feeding, dressing, and teaching them.

Fulfillment

The Lord has done great things for us, and we are filled with joy.

Psalm 126:3

As the twins grew, I longed for another baby. Jon and I headed to the fertility doctor and once again had to lean on God's infinite wisdom and believe that I would get pregnant with the exact baby or babies that he had chosen for us in his perfect timing.

For I know the plans I have for you, plans to prosper you and not to harm you, plans to give you hope and a future.

Jeremiah 29:11

God's Plans

m

o

Trust

Early in my pregnancy, when we learned I was carrying multiples, I felt insignificant and unworthy to mother so many children. As time passed we realized God did not make a mistake when he gave us six instead of just one. For us this was the beginning of learning to trust God completely.

Trust in the Lord with all your heart and lean not on your own understanding; in all your ways submit to him, and he will make your paths straight.

Proverbs 3:5-6

Being a "blob on bed rest" frustrated me because I could not adequately care for our three-year-olds. But then I realized that I was now a mom who was balancing the needs of eight children! Cara and Mady needed me to provide physical care while my unborn babies needed me to rest.

Struggles

Be still, and know that I am God

Psalm 46:10

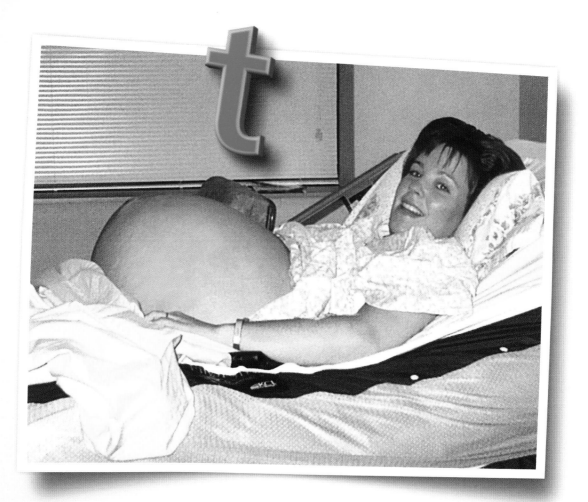

So much of my pregnancy with the six was about the medical aspect: what tests I needed; how many calories I was eating. Occasionally, though, I was able to reflect on what was happening. Who were all of these little people? Having them so close to me, I learned each of their personalities— even before they were born. Although we already had names chosen for each one, we waited until delivery day to assign them their own.

For you created my inmost being; you knit me together in my mother's womb. I praise you because I am fearfully and wonderfully made.

Psalm 139:13-14

Reflection

Motherhood

The long-awaited day had finally arrived. This was the day God had chosen to make me a mother to six additional children. What an amazing (and scary) responsibility!

Children are a heritage from the Lord, offspring a reward from him. Like arrows in the hands of a warrior are children born in one's youth. Blessed is the man whose quiver is full of them.

Psalm 127:3-5

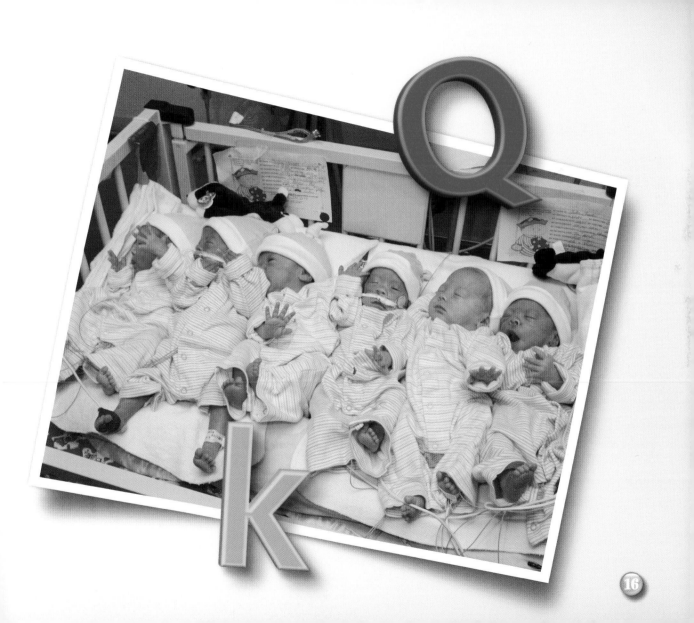

With the arrival of six more children, our most basic provisions were difficult. Jon was unemployed, and for the first time we had to ask for help. When we finally gave our worries to God, miraculous things happened and ultimately all of our needs were met.

Provision

Cast all your anxiety on him because he cares for you.

1 Peter 5:7

Because I was one mom caring for eight children all day, every day, I quickly realized that I was not enough on my own. I needed big doses of God-sized strength to get me through each day! One particularly exhausting day, my devotion included 2 Corinthians 12:9. I screamed out loud as God reminded me that his strength would be enough to get me through today ... and tomorrow ... and the next day.

My grace is sufficient for you, for my power is made perfect in weakness.

2 Corinthians 12:9

Strength

K 8

Joy

As a mom, there is nothing like walking from room to room, bed to bed, and watching my sleeping children. What joy to look at their peaceful, angelic faces as they dream of the day's events ... or maybe of that puppy they want so badly!

May the God of hope fill you with all joy and peace as you trust in him.

Romans 15:13

Sending my children off to school to be in the care of others is scary! Each morning as my twin girls get on the bus, I whisper a short prayer asking God to watch over them and bring them home safely. Then I leave my worry at his feet and trust him.

Security

Peace I leave with you; my peace I give you. Do not let your hearts be troubled and do not be afraid.

John 14:27

At the end of every long day, I always feel "mommy guilt" coming on! Thoughts of "I didn't get to play enough with them" or "I responded wrong in that situation" come to mind. I comfort myself in knowing that tomorrow is a new day with a fresh start of its own.

The steadfast love of the Lord never ceases; his mercies never come to an end; they are new every morning.

Lamentations 3:22-23 (ESV)

New Beginnings

I enjoy being Mom with Jon by my side as Dad. Over the years, I've seen our relationship grow and change as we figure out our roles and what works in our house. He is my balance, my strength, and my stability.

I thank my God every time I remember you.

Philippians 1:3

Unity

G

a

As a mom, I am faced with discipline issues daily—and sometimes hourly! In each situation I have the choice to respond in anger or to step back and ask God for his wisdom. I am not perfect and fail often, but my goal is to use every scenario to mold my children into the people God wants them to become.

Wisdom

By wisdom a house is built, and through understanding it is established; through knowledge its rooms are filled with rare and beautiful treasures.

Proverbs 24:3-4

There's no one recipe for love! Love is why I do everything I do for my children, like staying up until midnight baking cookies or putting notes in their lunches. Love is caring about every facet of who each one is and will become.

Whoever does not love does not know God, because God is love.

1 John 4:8

Many mornings my to-do list makes me feel defeated before my feet even hit the floor. The laundry piles are too big, there are too many bills to pay, meals to make, errands to do. Often I want to throw in the towel and say, "I surrender!" I could do that, or I could refuse to quit this all-important job called mothering.

Let us not become weary in doing good, for at the proper time we will reap a harvest if we do not give up.

Galatians 6:9

Perseverance

I often say, "If I don't laugh, I'll cry," and I mean that literally. Having the ability to see the humor versus the inconvenience or mess makes life more liveable ... and it creates many unforgettable memories!

Humor

A happy heart makes
the face cheerful,
but heartache crushes
the spirit.

Proverbs 15:13

Jon and I have learned that we don't want to be anywhere but where God wants us to be. We earnestly seek his direction and plan for our lives. And although our schedules are jam-packed, we know that he is with us, guiding our way.

Guidance

Your word is a lamp to my feet and a light for my path.

Psalm 119:105

h

Family

Around the dinner table each evening as I look from one face to the next, I realize what it means to be a family. I often tell my children, "Look around; these are, and will always be, your best friends."

Out of his fullness we have all received grace in place of grace already given.

John 1:16

Contentment

I have finally realized through this whirlwind that has been the last four years of my life that contentment is a choice. It's not what I have or don't have; it's an attitude. It's seeing the good in my life and then choosing to be content—even when times are tough and days are exhausting!

I have learned to be content whatever the circumstances. I know what it is to be in need, and I know what it is to have plenty. I have learned the secret of being content in any and every situation.

Philippians 4:11-12

I cannot say that I ever dreamed of becoming a mom to eight little faces, eight big personalities ... eight amazing children! Now that I am here, I feel more blessed than I deserve, more loved than I had hoped, and more content than I thought possible. To God be the glory indeed!

Now to him who is able to do immeasurably more than all we ask or imagine, according to his power that is at work within us, to him be glory ... forever and ever! Amen.

Ephesians 3:20-21

Blessings

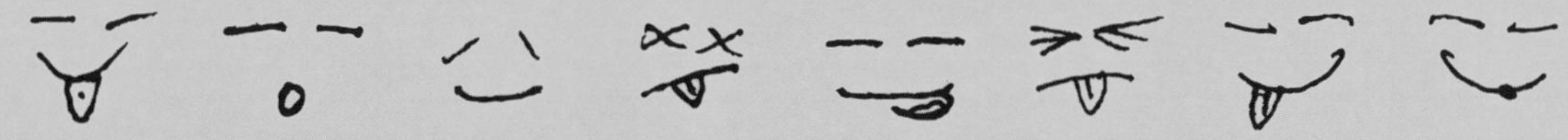

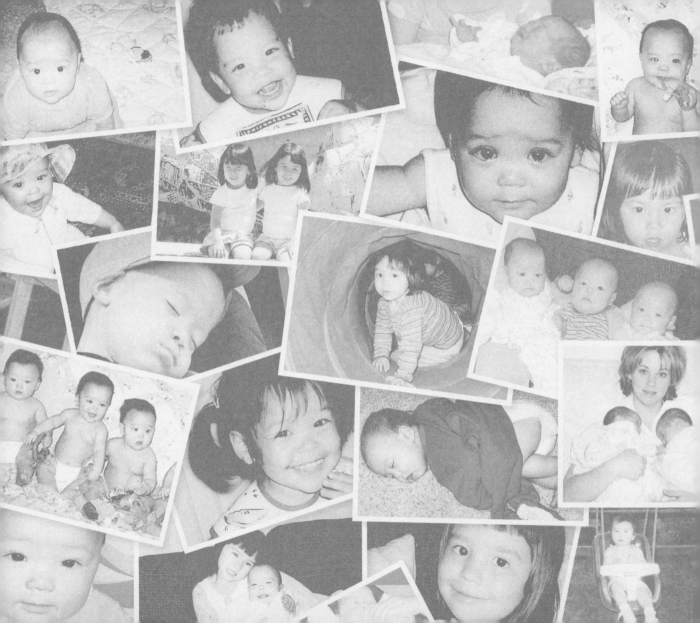